© 2020 Big River Publishing Brand.

Yukon de Leeuw
Look! A Life of Poetry
All rights reserved. No part of this publication may be reproduced, stored in a retrieval system or transmited in any form or by any means, electronic, mechanical, photocopying, recording or otherwise without the prior permision of the publisher or in accordance with the provisions of the Copyright, Designs and Patents Act 1988 or under the terms of any licence permitting limited copying issued by the Copyright Licensing Angency.

Published by: Big River Publishing Brand

Cover Design by: Yukon de Leeuw

A CIP record for this book is available from the Library of Congress Cataloging-in-Publication Data

ISBN-13: 978-1-7771690-0-8
Distributed by: Big River Publishing Brand

BISAC: POE011000

i'd like to dedicate this book to me
because i love me...
fully...
finally.

Look!
A Life of Poetry

By Yukon de Leeuw

Look! A Life of Poetry

table of contents

introduction...7
the child..9
the adolescent...31
the soldier..65
the senator..91
the philosopher...115

Introduction

I'm somewhat obsessed with autobiographies. I love reading the life stories of great people in their own words; the mind-sets and events that mystically steered them towards spectacular accomplishments. I'd often lie awake at night dreaming about my own autobiography and how it would read. What would I accomplish? What would the foreword say about how amazing I am? Then I got to my 25th circle around the sun and decided it's time to stop dreaming and time to start acting, literally and metaphorically.

Another obsession of mine is the human experience; more specifically human behaviour, psychology and culture, but I didn't realize the full extent of it until I started studying acting. We are magnificent creatures aren't we? Our relationships, ideas, nuanced personalities and histories make each of us an object of endless investigation. The best part is that we can observe ourselves—the most fascinating of concepts! So upon my new drive to tell my life's story, and my new found love for acting, I decided to start writing an autobiography — of sorts. The problem was I haven't lived long enough to justify an autobiography, I'm no Barak Obama. Even though I have had a plethora of experiences thus far, (an unusual amount for someone my age it seems) I'm still growing and my best years are still ahead of me. With that resolution I came to the decision that I ought to wait to write a formal autobiography.

Determined as I was to make something of myself, I started reflecting about my passion for music, lyrics and ultimately words. I started opening my old notebooks filled with poems, songs and journal entries. A lot of the material in this collection comes from ideas I had written down, or held in my immediate consciousness since childhood (this will be apparent in the first two parts). It's been a therapeutic process getting my ideas out on paper, something I continue to practice in my brightest and darkest hours.

To solve the problem of being a young adult attempting to write a full life's story, I would organize my poems in categories depicting each stage of life from birth to death. Through my training as an actor I discovered that I had a knack for putting myself in someone else's shoes, or even their mind/consciousness. I've been blessed with a close family, which has members occupying every stage of life. Through them, and through observations of my own experience I was able to write a full life's story. I'm sure if I wrote this book a decade earlier or later it would be entirely different, but alas, the idea struck me in this moment and so I must follow the feeling and write!

So there you have it; somewhere between a life story and a self-help book of free verse poetry, I've finally done it, I wrote my autobiography, or at least an abstract version of one. I hope you find this collection relatable in all it's glory and dis-ease.

The Child

Part 1: The Child

The Child

times are simple as a child,
but full of questions.

children are philosophers in their own right.

is doing the wrong thing
for the right reason
right?

free will/intentions

The Child

without barriers
expressions run wild.
a timeless ideal
rarely retained.

Yukon de Leeuw

life's a dream

try for a moment
to look at the world
through the eyes of a child,
really try.

see everything for the first time:
the faces with holes that hold eyes
that make soothing or sore sounds,
the gentle warm giants that cradle you,

the up that's light then dark,
the down that's cold then hot,
the in that's full then empty,
the out that's here then not.

what you'll see is life as a dream,
full of unseen powers and laws of physics.
pleasure and pain is all that exists.
has anything really changed?

The Child

pain

pain is an indicator
that something has to change
it's up to me to make it

for example:
relieve my bowels.
feels good
doesn't it?

what's the meaning of life?

what a silly question,
to be alive of course.

but what is being alive?

The Child

energy
energy is energy
the universe doesn't discriminate

my love
could be your hate
but the universe doesn't discriminate

mom

i saw my mom yesterday
for the first time
as a person
separate from myself.

she doesn't belong to me,
nor i to her.
her head is full of thoughts
outside of my existence.

all day she is thinking,
what could she be thinking?
it can't all be about me,
she's got her own things.

how strange,
suddenly her face changed
right before my eyes.
she caught me staring.

she asked:
"what?"
i said:
"oh, nothing."

The Child

    dad's purple soup

    give me a bowl of dad's famous purple soup.
    it doesn't look very good and it smells off too.
    but it's good for your bones and your heart and your soul,
        so pull out that ladle and dish me up a bowl!

    mmmm, sits well in my tummy
    and after a few spoonfuls it's kind of yummy!
    now i'm ready to run and play,
        i can't wait to have dad's purple soup another day.

a children's song

how would a horse play piano?
it's got big goofy hooves.
how would a bear play guitar?
it's got big sharp claws.
how would an elephant play the flute?
it's got a nose like a tube.
wait a minute
how would a human do that too?

ba-dum-bum-bum-bum

The Child

the babbling boobaly bop

the babbling boobaly bop
likes to talk a lot
it makes a bunch of noise
what it says? i know not.

the babbling boobaly bop
spins like a top.
it crashes through life
without a single thought.

the babbling boobaly bop
steams like a pot,
makes a big fuss,
complains and gets taught.

don't be a babbling boobaly bop.
stand for something more than not.
take responsibility
be a man.

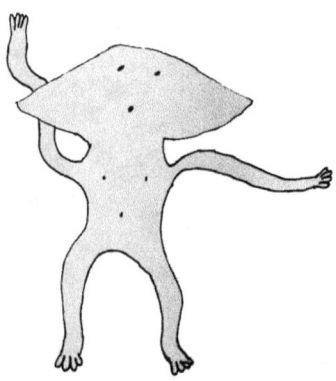

no pressure

i will be strong
i will have big muscles
i will be successful
and own lots of things

i will have a big family
all in a big house
it has a big pool
big toys and tools

i'm the last of my name
no pressure they say
but i should pass it on
to another male one day

The Child

here's a thesis statement on innocence:

to what extent do the external pressures placed upon an individual to transition into adulthood destroy that which is most sacred in them? or is the pressure itself natural and all the minute deaths purposeful? after all, the conceiving of, and utilization of these pressures evolved from the same deep space that birthed our race in the first place, as is the opposition, the resistance to these pressures.

in conclusion, conflict is natural.

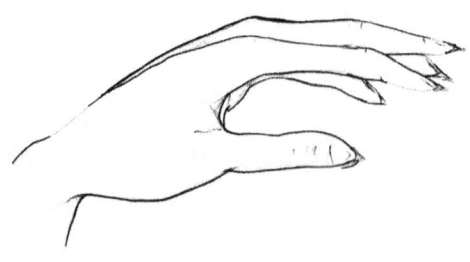

parents

imagining myself a force
spearing through this space.
i require resistance
or else i'll aimlessly pace.

The Child

here's an exercise:

put your two middle fingers together tip to tip, palms facing down. now let your hands go limp. now do it again, put your two middle fingers together, but this time apply strong consistent pressure between the two fingertips. maintain the pressure and let your hands go limp. the fingers stay afloat. this simple exercise demonstrates how a force requires a resistant force in the opposite direction to stay upright. such as the wing of an airplane requires air resistance to fly.

a metaphor if you will.

night terror

i have bad dreams
i run to my parents' bed
one day i need to stop
that's what they said.

i need to grow up
sleep alone in my head
will these nightmares go away
or do we just get used to them?

The Child

people

people are goofy
people are silly
people are ugly
people are pretty

people make movies
people make tunes
people make buildings
people make tombs

people are smart
people are dumb
people drink coffee
people drink rum

*people like people
and some people don't
i know those people
and i don't like them*

people are good
people are bad
people are happy
people are sad

people are humans
people are dogs
people are dolphins?
people are hogs

the world has people
the world is in space
space has aliens
we're an alien race!

blowing bubbles in milk

all the bubbles need to work together
if they want to reach the sky.
if one alone by itself tries
it gets too big, pops and dies.

The Child

a battery

i always follow my heart, my gut,
because that's our connector to god.
often the mind will get us stuck
when it thinks it knows better than god.
lol

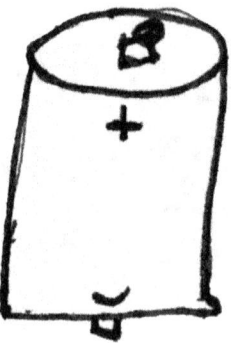

older

i wish i was older
big kids are so cool
they can do what they want
and don't have any rules.

but parents are too old
they don't have any fun
all they do is work
and wish they were young.

is anybody happy?

The Adolescent

Part 2: The Adolescent

The Adolescent

slides used to be fun
not this one
what's happening to me?
it's like i'm being squeezed

claustrophobia

;fsdjiafjifaoihag'ga'er9uag;inoar-
nop;fe'graeodifgh;odfha;nue
oener;niaegrn;igr;psr;ae-
grnjjm499pvyv5jy;pmhjsfjfsjldfsjlfdsjlk
dfsjkfaj;fajfeji;efjfae;lfesijaef;ja-
feijn;gijg09q0je;nuqvu;anut0948
aupweontvunpet8gjrb;n9q43nut-
vqpea9rogia923ita'nw[8[tnw4t]
;oaverutq93]b4qw;otibqu[3409ubep'9tuvnq
asdfsasdfasdfasgqwjpd
[4vntu9q[9e40ueiorj   cdf394u]tqn0t[egawp4o-
tye;roudsfafgfdgasdffa **me** kljjkyeor9yu[bw9e5uy[
9eragjdkfgn;lsdfasdfasd   fffferdfdfdasdf-
fljhjbkasfdfasdfdfjg;iaeijr   ;tbiaue'tp9
34ut';eoiruniowrjydfasdfa   asdfasasd-
fasdfdfsdjr'ynrupouyape9uyv95ua'dngobu
aery'bwenruy9uren[byuskjghwn]4-09qbu349q39-4tu'ard
aruy95u[0bq9wuer'pojdfkbnsjeuq;39u46-1u34-y=erh;idf

love and sex
sex and love
it hurts so good
i want it so bad
I must navigate thus

                                        social hierarchy
                                            i need to fit in
                                      i need to stand out
                                      to fit in. which is it?
                                   I must navigate thus

The Adolescent

a prepared speech

hey,
i just wanted to say a few things
so there's no confusion.
i'm afraid.
you may have noticed me acting strange,
and maybe caught me staring.
i hope i haven't offended you
it's just i think you're crazy beautiful.

it's not just because you're pretty

it's not just because you're pretty
its because you're a good person
and good people are attractive
thus being why you're pretty

it's not just because you're pretty
it's because you're smart
and smart people are attractive
thus being why you're pretty

it's not just because you're pretty
it's because you're strong
and strong people are attractive
thus being why you're pretty

it's not just because you're pretty
it's because you're wise
and wise people have a twinkle in their eye
thus being why you're pretty

it's not just because you're pretty
you go deeper than the surface
is what i've been trying to say.
but dang it you are pretty!

The Adolescent

please
for the love of God
don't say maybe.

fame

    i lied about losing my virginity
                              twice
    i really wasn't fooling anyone,
                            trust

    i was searching for just a hint of
                            fame
    but all i found was
                    shame

outdoor cat

i'm an outdoor cat
wandering the block,
people want to chat
what are they talking about?

don't look at my face
i'm not the mona lisa.
i lick my own fur
and eat my own feces.

people want to poke me
i am not an app,
people want to pet me
i am not all that.

sure i'm a little different,
but then again who isn't?
i sleep alone most every night
because i need to.

i'm an outdoor cat
wandering the block.
people want to chat
what are they talking about?

animal

having bits between your legs
can be so awfully annoying.
some days all i do is eat
and i still can't quench my appetite.

it's the animal in me that i can't control,
it's the nature in me that takes its toll,
it's a fine line between right and wrong,
i'm an animal after all.

~~there's got to be a better way~~

The Adolescent

this inner drive to procreate is killing me
it's killing me
how ironic

imagination
is far more extravagant
than reality could ever be.
but reality is better
because it actually happens
and when it does happen
it's magic.

just like imagination

The Adolescent

a soliloquy

an obsession, its become my water,
water at the bottom of a well.
my face reflected
at the bottom of the pool.

a cherry blossom floats down, its soft pink skin
blushing at me, inviting me in.
the urge to dive in hits, it would be my death
but how do i know i'm not already dead?

how do we know we're not already dead?

bone on bone

living together is tricky,
so is living alone,
proof that we need balance,
can't be bone on bone.

cartilage between us
to make the joints run smooth,
this way we'll be frictionless
doing what we do.

i'll make some mistakes,
about to be un leveled,
but i believe evolution,
i don't believe in heaven.

so feed my lilies when i'm gone
and clean up before i'm home.
i will do the same for you
because we can't be bone on bone.

living together is tricky,
so is living alone,
proof that we need balance,
can't be bone on bone.

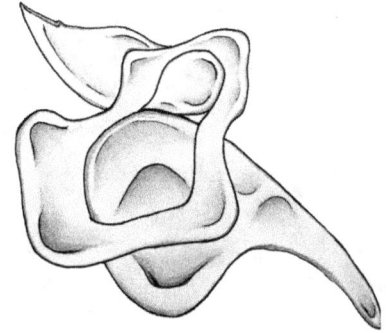

The Adolescent

```
                                    ,,,........::::::++++..
                  -............,,,,,,,,::::::\\\/////--------
                                                        ...
         ..."///...."""""///////////_____++++
            ...   ......"""""""""""""""""""""=========------
         ....,,,,......."                    """""""""  ......
         ............,,,,,,,,......   """"""""""""""""""""",,,,,,  ,,,,""
         ..::   '        .,,,,    ./ / / /          ..       - .
         . ....... ..;;;;  ,,,,,,,,   ,,,,,,,,,,,,,."""""  .    dream journal
```

your name comes up an awful lot in my journal.
i'm trying to work through these things
but these things—these feelings—
they seem to be winning.
.....'+++
=

the moon

i was looking at the moon;
thought you might be looking at it too,
but maybe it meant something different to me
than it did to you.

```
.............................................,,,,,,,,,,,,,,
,,,,,,,,,,,,,,,,,,,,,,,,,,,,,,,,,,,,,,,,,,,,    ........,,,,,,
-----------------============",,,,,,,,,,,,,,,,,,,,,,...
+++_____\\\\\\\\\\\\\\\\\\\",,,,,,,......
...
    ===+++++---------------\\\\\\\///::::::,,,,,,,,...
    .......................................---------\///......
                       ....................
                       ,,,,,,,,,,,,,,,,,,,,,,,........
',,,,,,,,,,,,
                    ...............,,,,,,,,,,,,,,,,,,,,,,
==+++++",,,,,,,,,,,,,,,"//
+++'.....
=
```

The Adolescent

the hurricane

a hurricane came over me
and pushed me to my knees.
it felt so heavy, i couldn't breathe.
i let go, i cried.

i felt the weight dissipate, i was light as fire.
i felt the heat leave my body, i was so tired.
i couldn't stand,
i cried some more.

i was already transcending.
my body couldn't hold that of me which wasn't physical.
i'm in the atmosphere,
i cried some more.

thankful for this pain i felt,
which learned me this lesson:
i am more than my name,
i am a hurricane.

video games
are so real.
maybe they are real
and maybe we're God.

with all this control!

The Adolescent

i think we need to let it be.

                                        there's two sides to every story.

i'll meet you in the middle.

                we'll get there when we get there.

shopping list

-kind
-considerate
-thoughtful
-active
-sense of humor
<u>-cares about me</u>
-adventurous
-brave
-good taste
-strong communicator
-ambitious
-knows herself
-charismatic
-positive
-not co-dependent
-not independent
-ariana grande

The Adolescent

indecisive

i'm so smart i'm confused,
hot and indecisive.
i'm so simple i'm certain,
full of conviction.

i can be deep,
        shallow,
                whole,
                        hollow.

i can be what i want to be
or i could be me for you.
all i really want is freedom
but too much and i'm gone for good.

if you chose me
i would be a lucky guy,
but it seems that you're afraid,
either that or you can't decide.

i guess i'll have to keep moving.

The Adolescent

endless

distractions seem justified.

i have an imposter syndrome:

something new becomes ordinary.

there will always be a horizon.

not all those who wander are lost…but i am

and that's ok

The Adolescent

iKnow

i know there's someone out there
who's just as lost as me.
if we can find each other
maybe we can find ourselves.

or vice versa

highs

i'm so high right now
i don't want to come down,
but you know what they say
about going up and coming down...

it makes me think of a frequency

The Adolescent

like when you're happy,
so happy,
    you laugh,
        you cry,
salt water comes out of your eyes

                        and when you're sad,
                            so sad,
                                      you

cry,

                                          you
                                      laugh,
                  salt water comes out like that

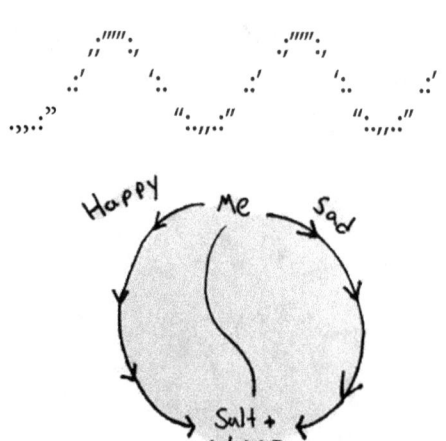

i was so happy when you called out my name.
so you can imagine how i felt
when you left me in the rain.

The Adolescent

me

i'm doing me
to the extreme
so that when we meet
she knows what she's getting herself into.

it only takes one

it's a grind,
but in the end
it only takes one.

one life
    one time
        one girl

it's out of my hands.
i couldn't possibly hope
to control that.

~~so realistically i should be able to relax.~~

The Adolescent

I had a dream last night
that we helped each other
achieve our wildest dreams

and then we went on vacation.

looking back

                                      we had a good thing.
                                            i can't believe
                                      it happened for me.

                  but somewhere we veered
              and when the clouds cleared
           a fork in the road was revealed.

i looked back
at what we were,
fondly.

The Adolescent

looks like you found someone.
good for you.
you look really cute together.
i'm fine.

i'm ross from friends

after all that
there's something i haven't asked...
how are you doing?
are you getting all the sympathy you need?

i'm not.

The Soldier

Part 3: The Soldier

The Soldier

how can i slow down?
i've got all these ways to grow.
leaving a trail of blood—
it's mostly my own.

masochist

it takes someone different
to be a musician.
i thought i was different,
but as it turns out
i'm the same as everyone else.

stolen dreams

The Soldier

sensitive boy

sensitive boy
i sense everything
sensitive boy
can't get a thing past me

sensitive boy
i cry at the movies
sensitive boy
girls think i'm a cutie

sensitive boy
i'm right in front of you
sensitive boy
i'm in the mirror too

sensitive boy
i sense everything
sensitive boy
can't get a thing past me

Yukon de Leeuw

all the things they thought i wouldn't,
i can, i could and i should.
i'm the youngest person to ever be me
so i might as well start right now.

The Soldier

chip, chip, chipping away
at an ice block day by day.
finally a figure protrudes,
a brave being bearing nude.

then the ice melts away,
the water flows
back into the bay
now what will you do?

do it again

i am a human

i will not be measured by the number of people i have slept with.
my marital status does not define me.
i will not be measured by the money in my bank account,
nor by the formal education i have completed,
and definitely not by the number of followers on my social media
accounts.

i will not be measured by my appearances,
not my height, not my weight
not my complexion and not the sound of my voice.
i will not be measured by my age,
because i have overcome a lot.
statistics will never measure me.

it's more a feeling

The Soldier

but a new generation is coming.
we feel differently
and so it will be
different.

be patient with us
the world will soon be ours

you know what the problem with your generation is?

                                              you're **entitled.**
      you feel entitled to an enjoy-full life
but joy is a privilege
not a right.

                    the **only** thing
                                    you are entitled to
is a life full
of experiences.

                nothing more

The Soldier

birth of the internet

bad news again online—
it kills me every time.
i have too much empathy—
it aches my insides

~~show me something good~~

actor on tv:

smokes a lot of cigarettes...
still has perfect teeth...

?

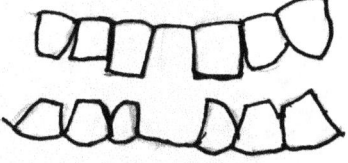

The Soldier

pretty people

pretty people on the tube
 doing simple things—
keeping us from ourselves
so we don't have to think.

Yukon de Leeuw

$

unquestioning loyalty
to the almighty dollar;
if it pays i'll play,
i have no standards.

The Soldier

marketing agencies:

designed to target my weaknesses,
to hit the core of my doubts,
telling me i'm not enough,
perpetuating the idea.

but i see you,
i see your intentions.
i see you!
so i win.

fear

stress is a disease
brought upon by fear
devastating to the body
and psyche.

fear is the best way
to control,
to exert power
if one lusts for more.

The Soldier

i can't seem to grow up,
i'm afraid i'm going to die young.
—
it's like there's a bear on my back,
i can't trust anyone.

depression joke

    you're not sick,
    you're lazy.
    go up stairs
      get
       some
        food
         in
          your
           belly.
    go outside
   feel the wind,
    feel alive
don't let them win.

The Soldier

when bad things happen i like to think
that it's saving my life from something worse in the
future.

Yukon de Leeuw

brother

you're like a brother to me.
even though you're not my real brother
i still love you
like you are.

we're not the ones to say i love you,
but if we were
know what i'd say?
i love you.

thanks for being there

shopping list pt.2

-meat
-tea
-soup

Yukon de Leeuw

how to be cool

this is a subjective world we live in.
it's cool not to care
what others think of you.

ironic isn't it

The Soldier

•

as we near the end
we have seen a new side of ourselves,
we have solved the problems that once burned our souls.
but like a circle
the end is also the beginning.

•

Yukon de Leeuw

    it's an early autumn this year—i don't mind—i've had enough summer it's time to fly; i'd rather be a bird in the sky than in a cage.
       this sense of security feels stale to me.
                      the certainty of survival bores me.
                            i'd rather live on the edge
                                          than in a cage.

The Soldier

pressure vol. 2

I can feel the pressure
angling my features,
the weight of experience
smoothing my skin,
sharpening my mind.
I do this all the time.

empirical wisdom
cannot be bought,
it must be earned
through attempts of grandeur
that often end with a spur
in the side.
I do this all the time.

oh

it feels good
ink gliding on paper
leaving my mark
leaving my skin.

to be a legend one must face demons,
demons and monsters,
the evil within.

one needs a break,
one being me.

The Soldier

today's an important day,
i don't know why
it just feels that way.

Part 4: The Senator

The Senator

i'm still a child;
i cannot fix the world,
but i can fix myself—
which is a world in itself.

first step:
be free

as it turns out
the meaning of life
is being in service to others.

The Senator

i am
grateful
for the fact
that i've been able to stay grateful
for being alive.

decisions are gifts
and not all are blessed
with the wherewithal.
decisions require responsibility.

responsibility terrified me

rock and roll is dead

rock and roll is dead.
they're speaking a different language these days.
it's just "me" and "i" and "my" and "mine"
and "you."

what ever happened to us?

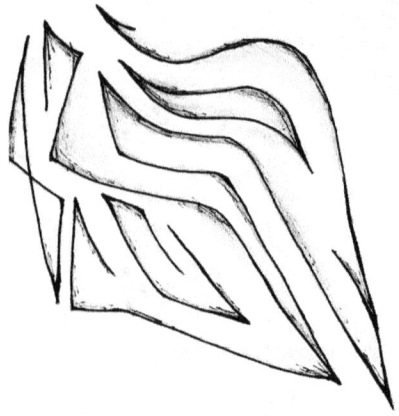

laws

some of them make sense,
some are means to an end,
and some are just incorrect.
history suggests they can be used to oppress.

it's a game played by the proprietors

The Senator

patriarchy

an innate desire
to build a benevolent empire.
are you with me or not?

                                        matriarchy

                    this queen of mine,
                     my partner in crime,
              we left the games behind.
            now the only game we play is:
      how do we best serve this community?

all it took
was some time apart
for me to realize
how special you are.

The Senator

this system favours the greedy,
but the universe does not.
capitalism is not the problem,
a problem solved is a problem lost.

greed is the problem

failure

we don't grow
if we don't struggle.
we boast success
and hide defects.
we could never win
if we've never lost.

*failing is the **BEST** progress.*

The Senator

i want to tell you about my failures

my failure at love,
how i became infatuated
and drove her away.

my failure as a son,
how i tried to impress
but couldn't obey.

my failure as a writer,
how i wrote a story
that now collects dust.

my failure as a musician,
how i made a song
that i can't stand the sound of.

my failure as an actor,
how i studied technique
but got caught up in industry.

my failure at peace,
how hard i fought
but in the end i lost.

it takes all kinds

who sets the stage?
the master of ceremony.
who sets the table?
the youngest child.

what does the farmer eat?
the fruits of his labour.
what does the tailor wear?
the threads of his labour.

when does the teacher learn?
when the student learns.
when is the artist inspired?
when the canvas is blank.

where does the carpenter live?
where ever he pleases.
where does the photographer look?
at moments in time.

why does the preacher preach?
to inspire.
why does the chorus sing?
to inspire—and to sing.

share the weight.

The Senator

patience

happily waiting,
waiting happily.
we have no choice
until we do.
*it is our greatest strength
until its cowardice.*

a modern person

-a modern person does not let anyone tell them who they are.
-a modern person adheres to their own values, but considers others.
-a modern person fights for what they believe in, but is **open** to new information.
-a modern person is versatile, fluid with the changing times.
-a modern person is honorable when speaking their mind.
-a modern person accepts their mistakes and learns from them.
-a modern person acknowledges their shortcomings, recognizes where they stem from and **works** towards a peaceful mind.
-a modern person sees and respects the tribulations of life.
-a modern person sees the strength in showing vulnerability.
-a modern person does not adhere to norms or stereotypes, but **understands** their truths.
-a modern person is not driven by selfish intentions.
-a modern person knows that they must take care of themself before they can take care of others.
-a modern person knows that what they don't know is far **more** important than what they do know.

-a modern person is as old as time.
-a modern person will forever be re-defined.

The Senator

meditate

pray, believe, religion,
3rd eye, 5th element, 4th dimension,
6th sense, science.

i'm attempting to understand that one thing,
that one thing that can't be understood,
only felt.

it's just too big, it goes too deep.
where we fit in will never be fully revealed.
we were meant to float in this abyss.

paradox

its a paradox.
what separates us
also brings us together.

like war,
peace,
life and death.

everything is divine—
divine in balance.
don't stress about a thing.

garbage rap

there's a whole lot of garbage around my place;
its always been that way.
it blows around, it rots, it packs,
it's food for the birds and rats.

it flies and swims,
it does everything.
born in a blink
lasting for infinity.

woah.

matter

everything breaks down:
shoes, mountains, bodies.
it's the nature of matter.
i won't feel bad
it's just a matter of nature.

The Senator

this next poem is based on some advice i heard

there's a difference between getting old
and growing old.

the latter trades youth for wisdom;
the former can't let go—gets none.

don't fight it.

ideas are infinity

these are borrowed ideas,
they're everlasting,
they're infinity.
infinity is as big small as it is big.
as big small as it is big!

it goes inwards as much as it does outwards.

The Senator

peace

it is my firm belief
that if you look hard enough
you can understand and relate
to every life.

Yukon de Leeuw

1knowledge

the desire for knowledge
for the purpose of power—
absent of love—
dies in vain.

to wonder and marvel,
to beckon change
is to be born again
when you die.

The Senator

a fun fact

as bipedal homo sapiens
we are the least efficient animals on earth,
but with the invention of the bicycle
we become the most efficient...

*innovation is how we've survived
and it's how we will continue to do so.*

Part 5: The Philosopher

The Philosopher

returning to dirt
a circle comes back around
we must tell this story
to bury in the ground

teaching is a learning process

Yukon de Leeuw

physical things
don't concern me
much

unless it has to do with beauty and grace...

The Philosopher

```
      ,,,,,..··"··......,,,              ,,,,,,,··"··......,,,,,
     /               \\ //                \
     |                love                  |
     |                                      |
        |                                |
        one did not give you the feeling
         they awakened it within you
           yes it was within you
                all along
                \\   //
                  '
```

These days
people talk about beauty
but what ever happened to grace?
Grace is everything.

the goldfinch brings joy

this life was meant for you son

  the chickadee can lower its body temperature by chirping

  the chickadee can lower its body temperature by chirping

  the chickadee can lower its body temperature by chirping

i don't know what it means yet, but i will soon...

The Philosopher

    i look at a crow   and wish i could play
      crow looks at eagl e   /^\   and wishes for the same
        eagle looks at flying   how we look at driving
                          utility
                        /mostly

fulfillment is a daily practice.
one single event won't fulfill me eternally,
it'll take consistent effort.

The Philosopher

a wasted song

i've wasted my money
i've wasted my time
i've wasted my savings
i've wasted my rights
i've wasted my dollars
i've wasted my life
chasing another man's life

each day i grow
older and wise
if god has a plan
i know i'll be fine

i've run over mountains
and riverbeds dry
to find it's the same
on the other side

i've wasted my money
i've wasted my time
i've wasted my savings
i've wasted my rights
i've wasted my dollars
i've wasted my life
chasing another man's life

one day i'll catch him
i know that i will
that pretty boy leo
and throw him in jail

i've jumped over ponds
i've jumped over seas
if it's all for nothing
that's fine with me

i've wasted my money
i've wasted my time
i've wasted my savings
i've wasted my rights
i've wasted my dollars
i've wasted my life
chasing another man's life

The Philosopher

the science of forgiveness

the science of forgiveness
has to be proven yet
but i'd put money
on all of its benefits.

forgive myself—
why's it so hard?
every detail
can be picked apart.

when i was young
building habits,
unconsciously i was
shaped an addict.

i'll start from scratch
at any age—
forgive myself
day after day.

"life is suffering"
the Buddhists say
"the cost of living,"
"the price we pay."

no matter the life
you can't escape,
unless maybe
you meditate?

The Philosopher

aspen grove

aspens need direct sunlight
they cannot grow at night
it would take a storm of some kind
to clear the shadows cast by pines

  a
strike
    of
lightning
    sparks
  a
    fire!
a forest burns to the ground

now what is ash
will soon be grown
into an aspen grove

life needs death

the healer

i saw them through the thicket
a subtle form wearing fur
they came in my direction
and i knew right then and there
that i would be okay.

they gave me food and juice to drink
although i don't have the sweetest tooth
it was like a dream before it hits
i didn't have the slightest clue
that this change in me would be
so i could heal another
because in that moment
i couldn't be bothered.

the healer knelt down
and lowered their tone
it was smooth as a baby's cheek
they told me to mind my health
because "you can't heal another
until you heal yourself."

i looked into their eyes, got lost in space,
a question rolled out of my face.
i asked the healer "why me? why now?
you could have been any other place."
they spoke not a word
just stood there a blur
and faded back into their fur.

The Philosopher

i almost died that night
out there in the woods
starved and burned
froze and shook
but i made it out
it was me they helped
i'll never forget how it felt.

i hope one day
i can return the favor
be there for someone else.

The Masculine and Feminine
are eternally different
one is fire the other water
one is not better than the other

they were borne on different planes
they cannot be compared
they cannot be the same
yet life exists between their eternal dance...

The Philosopher

like water

you will find the path of least resistance
but still there will be resistance.
it will be bountiful
for in the case of no resistance...

you would be still
like a puddle
in a ditch
growing old
and stinky.

a river however
is fresh and filtered
resistance from earth
keeps it clean.

so you must keep moving
through the resistance.
it's not breaking you,
it's cleansing you.

and fire

water doesn't care
where it's going
where its been
it never hurries
never worries

it's always where it needs to be.

a river never stops
but water evaporates.
a fire burns out
the heat dissipates

the fire flames flicker
just like the water splashes
it trickles and splinters,
but they can't coexist.

yet the intersect of both
gave birth to me.
not created
nor destroyed
i live in between.

The Philosopher

There's something deeply magical—religious about the two opposing energies that gave birth to life on earth. there's philosophical truths built into their natures.

if i may be so bold
to give some advice
it would be
don't undermine another's struggle

The Philosopher

let me explain

imagine the **2nd dimension,** such as when you take a picture. time doesn't exist in the 2nd dimension; therefore the objects occupying this dimension are stuck in space—unable to move. we are occupying the 2nd dimension at every individual moment that makes up time; however these moments are infinitely minute. all these moments put together become the 3rd dimension.

in the **3rd dimension** time does exist and allows us to travel through space at will. traveling through space takes time. in the 4th dimension, time can be traveled through—much like how space is in the 3rd dimension. seeing as we exist in the 2nd and 3rd dimension, part of us could exist in the 4th as well.

let's assume this to be true for argument's sake. if part of our soul/psyche/energy (for lack of a better term) occupies the **4th dimension,** and so does everyone else's, and since time is a malleable entity in the 4th dimension, that means our soul/psyche/energy has lived in everyone and everything at one point or another. rather, *it is* living in everyone and everything, even right now as we speak.

we are **everything** that has ever existed, right now and forever.

maybe through that door is where we go when we die.

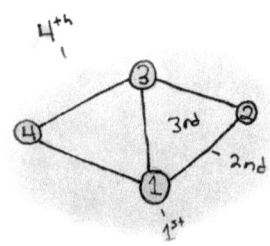

the mountain

all to be remembered, all to be forgot,
i found myself in a valley dark.
the alpine peaks were glowing,
the sun was setting showing
me that everything is temporary.

the climb was rough and rumble,
the summit is humble.
up here i can see it clear
why i had to struggle.

all to be remembered, all to be forgot,
i found myself where i got lost.
the alpine peaks were glowing,
the sun was setting showing
me that everything is temporary

now i'm looking down
back to where i was
i'm going just there
i know what needs to be done.

all to be remembered, all to be forgot,
i found myself just where i was.
the alpine peaks were glowing,
the sun setting showing
me it's all temporary.

The Philosopher

personality

the drive to be
alive and free
each experience
fused together

every little thing
that has ever happened
and is still happening
in one

that's me

knowing we will never know is knowing

we are a process
we are change
we never find us
we create us instead
we haven't happened
we happen yet
and knowing we'll never know
is knowing best.

The Philosopher

all we have is this exact moment

and now it's gone.
and now this one!
and now that's gone too.
and now this one!
and this one!
here comes another!
oops, you missed it
better luck next time

Yukon de Leeuw

listen here

if you were ready for there
you would already be there
but you're not there
you're here
so be here

and then maybe you'll be ready

The Philosopher

as it turns out
the meaning of life is
to ripple through time,
to pulse, to vibrate,
so that beauty
and god
and the great ether might exist.
so that we might catch a glimpse
of that beauty that we belong to
and that also belongs to us.

Yukon de Leeuw

having a drink looking out the window

having a drink,
looking out the window,
thinking back to when my life belonged to someone else...

i'm so grateful

leaving

we might have to leave home
we might have to fly away
but our energy is everlasting
it won't ever fade

grandpa

but then again what is real?
what's the difference
between reality and dreams
and memories?

it's getting harder
to decipher
which is which
i'm all of the above

i can fly
i'm in love again
until next time
goodbye friend

The Philosopher

a lot of people died to make this happen
a lot of pictures were taken on that phone
and now it's in the water
oh no

thank god for the cloud(s)

the ever elusive sleep

when will it come?
my entire life i've been waiting
to be taken under
just to wake
and do it again
tomorrow

and tomorrow
and tomorrow

The Philosopher

one

one thing i've learned
as i've gotten older
is that you never really get old
time just slows down
or speeds up
until you become one

and then you become one

thanks for spending some time with me :)

www.ingramcontent.com/pod-product-compliance
Lightning Source LLC
Chambersburg PA
CBHW070044120526
44589CB00035B/2314